Giraffe Weevil

by Grace Hansen

Abdo Kids Jumbo is an Imprint of Abdo Kids
abdobooks.com

abdobooks.com

Published by Abdo Kids, a division of ABDO, P.O. Box 398166, Minneapolis, Minnesota 55439.
Copyright © 2022 by Abdo Consulting Group, Inc. International copyrights reserved in all countries.
No part of this book may be reproduced in any form without written permission from the publisher.
Abdo Kids Jumbo™ is a trademark and logo of Abdo Kids.

Printed in China

052021

092021

THIS BOOK CONTAINS
RECYCLED MATERIALS

Photo Credits: Alamy, iStock, Minden Pictures, Science Source, Shutterstock PREMIER,
©Tee La Rosa p.15 / CC BY-NC-ND 2.0

Production Contributors: Teddy Borth, Jennie Forsberg, Grace Hansen
Design Contributors: Candice Keimig, Victoria Bates

Library of Congress Control Number: 2020947650
Publisher's Cataloging-in-Publication Data

Names: Hansen, Grace, author.

Title: Giraffe weevil / by Grace Hansen

Description: Minneapolis, Minnesota : Abdo Kids, 2022 | Series: Incredible insects | Includes online
resources and index.

Identifiers: ISBN 9781098207373 (lib. bdg.) | ISBN 9781644945575 (pbk.) | ISBN 9781098208219
(ebook) | ISBN 9781098208639 (Read-to-Me ebook)

Subjects: LCSH: Beetles--Juvenile literature. | Rain forest animals--Juvenile literature. | Insects--Juvenile
literature. | Insects--Behavior--Juvenile literature.

Classification: DDC 595.7--dc23

Table of Contents

Giraffe Weevils

Giraffe weevils are **native** to Madagascar. They live in the island country's eastern rainforests.

N
W E
S
Madagascar

Weevils are beetles with long snouts called rostrums. They have chewing mouthparts at the ends of their snouts.

rostrum

Different weevil **species** eat just one kind of plant. They get their name from the plant they eat. The giraffe weevil is different. It gets its name for its long neck!

The neck of a male giraffe weevil is longer than that of a female. Males use their long necks to fight. Females use their necks to build nests.

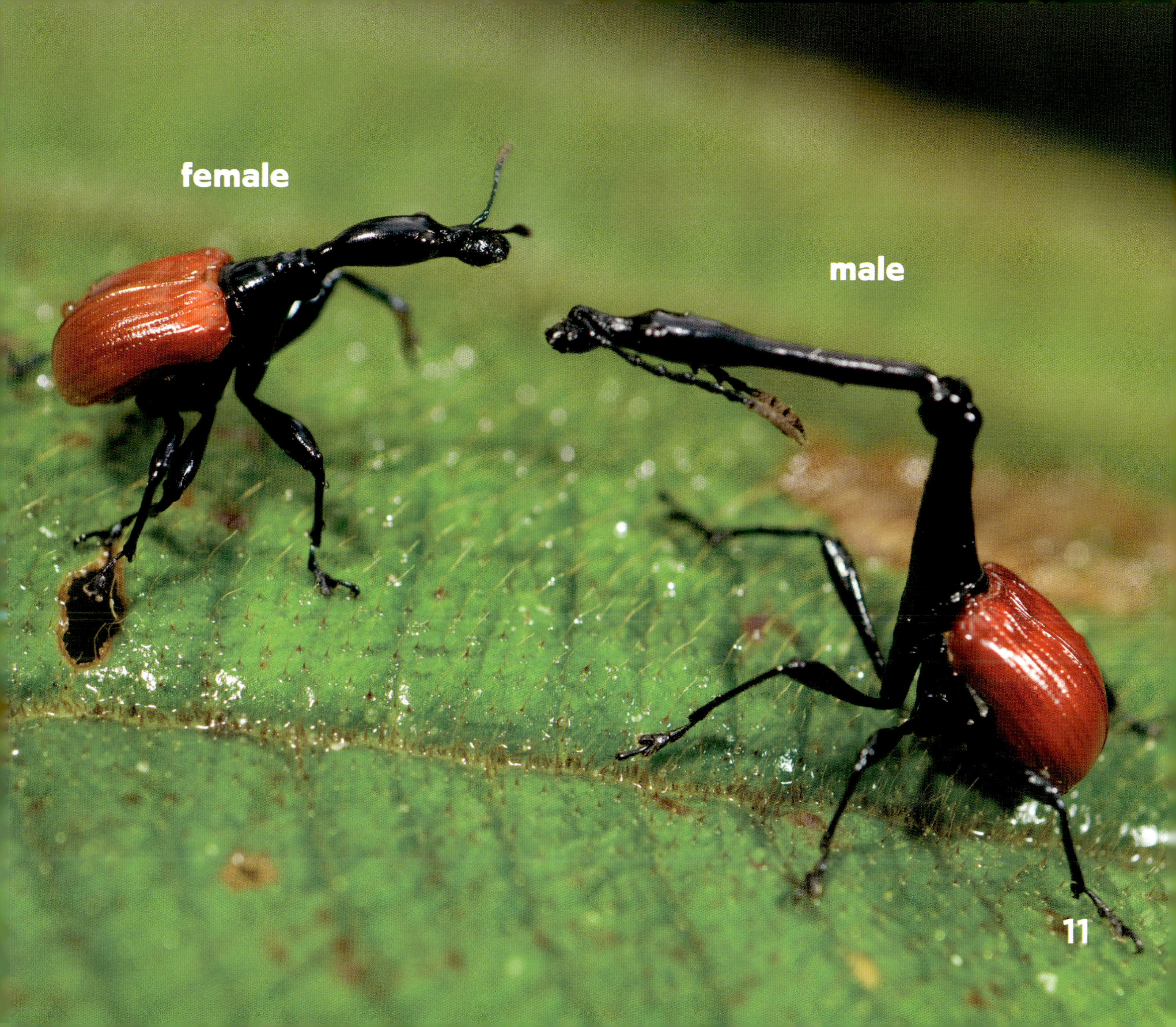
female
male
11

Giraffe weevils are mostly black in color. They have bright red **elytra** covering their wings.

elytra

Food

Giraffe weevils rarely leave the small tree they feed from. The tree is nicknamed the "giraffe beetle tree." It has green leaves and is only found in Madagascar.

Battling and Mating

When giraffe weevils are ready to **mate**, the males fight one another. The winning male gets to mate with a female.

The female uses her strong legs to fold the leaf of a giraffe beetle tree. She curls up the end of the leaf and lays one egg inside. She uses her neck and legs to roll the rest of the leaf up.

The female then snips the leaf off of the tree. It falls to the forest floor. When the egg hatches, the **larva** will have something to eat!

21

More Facts

- There are around 60,000 known weevil **species** in the world. But there are many more that have not been discovered!

- Giraffe weevils do not bite or sting.

- Madagascar is known for having unique species of insects, animals, and plants that aren't found anywhere else in the world. Giraffe weevils are just one of those special species.

Glossary

elytra – the pair of hardened forewings of certain insects, like beetles, that form a protective covering for the flight wings.

larva – an insect after it hatches from an egg and before it changes into its adult form. A larva does not have any wings and looks like a worm.

mate – to come together to have young.

native – belonging naturally to a place.

species – a group of living things that look very much alike, share a similar name, and can have young with one another.

Index

Visit **abdokids.com** to access crafts, games, videos, and more!